THE PAGE.

Page 12.

MY GOLDEN SHIP.

BY

MARY E. ROPES,

AUTHOR OF

"ONLY A BEGGAR BOY," "PRYING POLLY," "TILL THE SUGAR MELTS," ETC.

London:

THE RELIGIOUS TRACT SOCIETY,

56, PATERNOSTER ROW; 65, ST. PAUL'S CHURCHYARD;
AND 164, PICCADILLY.

CONTENTS.

MY GOLDEN SHIP.

CHAPTER I.

FRIENDS AND FOES.

THE brilliant summer sun was already descending towards the west, shining in at the back windows of the houses in the seaside town of East Wavebury, turning its dusty glass windows into molten gold, and lighting up the breezy downs that stretched far away inland, while in front—facing the sea—the rugged cliffs, stern in their pitiless outlines, stood in sullen shadow, as though cruelly anticipating the miserable fate of many a gallant craft upon the reefs at their base, where other noble vessels had already, in stormy winters gone by, been wrecked and lost.

At the door of a cottage near the edge of the cliff sat a lad busily mending a fishing-net, but finding time, now and again, to look across the expanse of sea before him, with lingering, loving eyes.

His sunburnt face was radiant with the bloom of health, and his deep grey eyes, as he gazed far out towards the horizon, were thoughtful beyond his years.

"Oh, isn't that lovely!" he exclaimed, as a ship, with all sail set, glided across the gold and crimson sea just where the tints fell most brightly, beyond the deep shadows cast by town and cliffs.

She was a stately vessel with pure white wings and shining figure-head; and as she sailed right into the glowing light, from stem to stern she was transfigured by a glow that seemed almost more than natural.

"She's just like a golden ship," said Charlie Walter to himself. " If there was to be any sea in heaven, I should say that such-like must be the look of the ships there."

Charlie, though only a fisher lad, had a keen eye for the beautiful, and to him the bountiful, generous sea, which yielded him a living, was an ever-changing world of beauty and interest.

"What are you a-thinkin' of, my boy ?" said a voice behind him, and Mrs. Walter's good motherly hand was laid upon the lad's shoulder.

For all answer, Charlie pointed to the ship, still gliding on with the gentle breeze, and still bathed in golden splendour.

" Yes, dear, I see. It's like a pictur'."

" I wonder, mother," said Charlie presently, dropping his net, and leaning his head for a moment against his mother's arm,—" I wonder if, when Jesus was in a ship on the Sea of Galilee, it looked like that sometimes!"

" I shouldn't be surprised, dear," replied Mrs. Walter.

" If so be it had been day instead of night,

that time when Jesus walked on the water,
and if the sea had been like this one now,
I shouldn't have wondered at Peter sayin',
' Bid me come to Thee on the water'; for it
looks like a golden road, mother, leadin' to
somewheres blessed.   But it was night, and
a rough sea, and everything to frighten
him, save that the Lord Himself was there."

There was silence for a few moments, for
mother and son were thinking, and during
these few moments the golden ship slipped
past the wondrous pathway of light, into the
cool grey tints beyond, and was golden no
more.   While just then, from the landing-
place at the pier,—unfurling her mainsail,
which was at once caught by the freshening
wind,—a gallant yacht shot out, and began
to skim and curtsey across the bay.

Charlie's keen sight enabled him to recognise the people on board.

" Ah!" said he, with a sigh, the dreamy,
happy look fading out of his face; " there
goes the young Squire in the *Sea Gull.* If
he don't lead an easy life of it, no one ever
did.   And that yacht, mother; why, they say
she's his very own, and he has four sailors
to look after her, and a master to sail her

beside, 'cause he himself don't know nothin'
about boats, and he's sea-sick even yet
when there's a bit of a breeze; such a
land-lubber!" and the young fisherman's
lips curled with something rather like a
mild form of contempt.

"Well, Charlie, that ain't his fault," said
Mrs. Walter. "No one would be sea-sick if
so be they could behave different; as your
father said to me the first time as ever I
went fishin' with him. We was courtin', you
know, Charlie; but, bless you, that's nothin'
agen sea-sickness, and I finished up by lyin'
in the bottom of the boat, all white and
green and yellow with that same sickness."

"Well, of course women is different,"
replied the lad. "Fishin' and sailin' ain't
their business; but for a young gent to be
sea-sick aboard of his own yacht is real
stupid."

"He'll get over it some day," said Mrs.
Walter, smoothing her boy's brow, upon
which a frown had gathered.

"But don't it seem hard, mother," said
Charlie again, after a pause, "that some folks
should have everything, and other folks
nothin'?"

" I don't know what you mean, Charlie."

" Well, mother, now there's the young Squire ; he's an only son, like me, and just look at him. Haven't he got everything that he can wish for ?   A yacht, and a horse to ride, and a pair of ponies for his basket carriage, and a groom all to himself, and as much money as he can spend ; and here's me with nothin'."

" Do you call it nothin', Charlie, that God has given you health and strength to earn a honest livin', and that you've them near you as love you dear and true, and in their humble fashion try their best to make you happy ?"

" Mother, mother darlin', I don't call that nothin' ; you know how I love father and you ; but somehow I feel kind of bitter now and then when I see the young Squire sailin' or drivin' by, and think what a easy life he has of it."

" Well, dear," responded Mrs. Walter, " of course I can't argufy the matter with you as the parson might ; but it do seem to me that those who wants to be like the Lord, and to have His Spirit in them, may well be content to be poor as He were, and to get their livin' out of the sea, as some of His disciples did. Them as truly loves Him, Charlie, tries to love their fellows, and there's no envy in real love."

Charlie did not reply except by pressing his mother's hand, showing thus that he understood her words, and confessed their truth.

Then he went on with his net-mending, and Mrs. Walter repaired to the kitchen to get the tea ready.

Perhaps Claude Rivington, the Squire's only child, was less to be envied than Charlie Walter thought. True, he had been accustomed to every luxury that a fond father could provide for him; but his mother had died some years ago, and his character, though really good in many ways, and not naturally selfish, showed the want of that influence and training which a mother can so often give.

Besides this, the boy was a sufferer from a chronic disease which at times caused him much pain, and almost always discomfort and weariness, so that often he could have wished to exchange lots with the rough, hardy, jolly fisher lads, who never seemed to have an ailment, and who needed not the luxuries of life to keep them healthy and happy.

But Charlie knew nothing of all this, so perhaps it was not wonderful that he should sometimes have had murmuring or envious thoughts, though he was too good a lad to suffer them to remain very long, and thus to sour his naturally sweet and contented temper.

"Charles Walter, our housekeeper have sent me to say that if your father should have any nice fresh fish to-morrow mornin', he can send or bring it up to the Hall."

Charlie looked up from the net he had completed mending, and saw that the speaker was the Squire's page, who had just walked up along the narrow cliff path. Very smart about the buttons, and very lofty about the nose was this page; for his buttons were bright and new, and his nose was cocked up in the air, to indicate the superior station and great condescension of the owner.

"Very well," replied Charlie, in no way impressed by the other's airs and graces. "Father's goin' out fishin to-night, and should he take anything worth sendin' up to the Hall, I'll bring it myself in the mornin'."

The page took himself off without replying to Charlie's civil good afternoon. He evidently resented being made the messenger to a fisherman's cottage, and therefore would exchange only as few words with Charlie as was absolutely necessary. It was not the first time he had been sent, for the house-keeper at the Hall was an old acquaintance of Mrs. Walter, and quite as much for her friend's sake as for the sake of procuring what she could depend upon as fresh fish, she often sent the page or any one of the Hall servants who might be coming into the town, with an order.

John Walter and his son were out all night, taking a better haul than usual, and while John was arranging with the dealer who bought up fish every day for the London market, Charlie, carrying a basket of the choicest specimens, set off to walk to the Hall, a distance of about a mile and a half, along the cliff road.

As he passed by a cutting which led down by a steep rocky path to the beach below, he saw two men sitting close together on a stone at the top, and evidently in earnest conversation. As they looked up at him, he recognized Black Darley and Crafty Joe, as they were commonly called; two fishermen who were rather shunned by the rest of the fisher-folk, for in time past they had been suspected of dishonesty in various ways. There were whispers of their having given help to smugglers on the coast; and once they had even been accused of house-breaking, though they could not be convicted, on account of the evidence being incomplete.

Charlie was passing them without taking any notice, when Black Darley called out, "I say, young master, be you bound for the Hall?"

"Yes," replied Charlie, and was going on, but Crafty Joe jumped up and caught him by the arm.

"Not so fast, Charles Walter," said he. "You ain't in such a hurry but what you can answer a few questions, I suppose?"

Charlie did not reply.

"Now then," said Black Darley, "is them fish an order from the Hall?"

"Yes," answered Charlie, "and as I'm late

anyway, I'll ask you to let go my arm, Joe Slide."

"Time enough; don't you be in such a hurry," sneered Joe, still keeping his hold. "I say, Darley, don't it seem as if the Hall kind of favours them Walters? *We* gets no orders from the Squire, no, nor shouldn't, I believe, if we was to go down on our knees for 'em."

"You don't do much fishin'," replied Charlie boldly. "No one can't live on orders, if there's nothin' to supply them with. And sitting at the top of a cuttin' ain't the best way to earn a livin'."

"Now look here, none of your imperence!" snarled Black Darley. "'Tain't your business whether we works or not, and this high road ain't a pulpit, nor yet you the parson."

"Well, we all knows that," put in Crafty Joe; "no offence meant, Charles Walter, so don't take none. But as you're up at the Hall so often (and a fine old place it is, to be sure) you must know every nook and corner of it, and could tell us lots of interestin' things."

"I don't know nothin' worth repeatin',"

replied Charlie, "and if I did I wouldn't tell either of you."

"Softly, softly," said Joe, winking slyly at his companion; "don't you take on so, Charlie; Darley and me is the last men what would ask you to blab. It was only a slip of the tongue that come out unbeknownst like. The truth is we're both a little sore that the Hall don't help us poor folk more. Here's Squire Rivington just rollin' in money, and his son goin' round and lordin' it like a young prince; and here's us as has to earn our livin' by the sweat of our brow. So we says, says we, 'Why should he have everything and us nothin'?'" And a dark frown settled down upon the speaker's brow, and was reflected on that of his companion.

Charlie started, and looked in conscience-stricken horror at the faces before him.

Yes, these were almost his own words to his mother the day before. This dark and evil frown was the sign of envy and discontent—feelings which he had too often cherished in his own heart.

But what a hateful, horrible passion this envy appeared now! How different from what he had ever felt it to be before. Could anything be more wicked, more un-Christ-like ?

There had been a short silence, during which thoughts and feelings like these had filled the mind and heart of Charlie Walter. Then Black Darley broke the pause by saying, " I hear the old Squire's away just now ; ain't he ? "

" I don't know," replied Charlie.

" Is it a nice house ? As nice as they say ? " asked Crafty Joe, with a sudden change of manner and a smile intended to be winning, but which was not much more so than a hyena's laugh. " Tell us, Charlie," he continued, " is it a fine house, with heaps of servants, and lots of furniture and silver, and everything on the grand ? "

" Lots of silver, eh ? " repeated Darley. " And pray where do they keep it ? "

But Charlie was neither to be frightened nor cajoled into answering even those ques-tions to which he could have replied.

" I told you afore," said he, firmly, " that I wasn't goin' to answer your questions, so the sooner you let me go the better for you and me both."

B

"There, then, get along with you for a obstinate, pig-headed boy!" cried Black Darley savagely, while Joe only growled and scowled and muttered some inaudible words.

On his way to the Hall along the pleasant cliff road, however, after he had left the men at the cutting, Charlie was overtaken by Claude Rivington who was driving his pair of ponies, and for once had no groom with him.

Charlie could not help noticing the young Squire's wan cheek and dull heavy eyes; and the feeling of envy which had just been rebuked by a glimpse of the same evil spirit in Black Darley and Crafty Joe, gave place to a feeling akin to compassion for the lad so near his own age, to whom even a yacht and a pair of ponies could not bring red cheeks and bright eyes, and the zest in mere living that comes to the thoroughly healthful.

Claude pulled up as he came abreast of Charlie, and said, "You're Charles Walter, are you not?"

"Yes, sir, that's my name."

"Are you going up to the Hall?

"Yes, sir; the housekeeper ordered some fish, and I am takin' it up."

"Can you tell me who those two men are whom I passed just now?"

"Sittin' at the top of Stony Cutting, sir? Their names are Blake Darley and Joe Slide, but they're known better as Black Darley and Crafty Joe."

"I could not help noticing them," said Claude, "because they eyed me so strangely, and whispered and muttered to each other as I passed. They looked really as though they hated me, and I'm sure I have never done them any harm."

Again Charlie felt the sting of self-reproach. Again he considered that after all it was but envy that these men had felt towards one better off than they were; and had not he himself been guilty—though perhaps in a smaller degree—of that same envy, that same discontent? Had not he, Charlie Walter, sinned this same sin, in spite of all his advantages, in spite of all his careful training, and of the peace and happiness that had made his humble lot so sweet?

"No, sir, I'm sure you've never done nothin' to make them feel so," said Charlie in reply; "but they're idle fellows as don't choose to work, and think they ought to be kept by those as is richer than theirselves."

"That's extremely unreasonable," said Claude; "they would be just about the last people one would care to assist."

"Yes, sir, that's quite right," replied Charlie."

"Well, I suppose I'd better be trotting on," said Claude. "Good morning, Charles Walter;" and touching the off pony with the whip he turned down a cross road leading inland, and was soon out of sight.

CHAPTER II.

AGATE BAY.

FEW days after this conversation between the two boys, Claude himself called one morning, on horseback, at the cottage. He did not dismount, but John Walter happened to be at home, and to him Claude explained the reason for his coming. One of the sailors belonging to his yacht was ill, and he begged that Charlie might be allowed to fill his place.

"I don't go sailing every day," added the young Squire, "and when the *Sea Gull* is at anchor your son can be with you, or do anything he chooses. Only I should like him to accompany the yacht when she sails."

John demurred a little, but at last gave

his consent; and that very afternoon Charlie found himself on board the *Sea Gull*, skimming lightly over the waves, and vastly enjoying his new and easy duties.

The wind was pretty fresh, and Claude, although not actually sea-sick, was not yet sufficiently accustomed to the motion of the vessel to feel very comfortable. So he wrapped himself in a rug, and lay down on a pile of cushions on deck close by the cabin door, and when Charlie was passing, he called him and said : " If you haven't anything particular to do, Charles, I should like to have a little chat with you."

" No, sir, I've nothin' to do just now; I can stay for a bit."

" Well, then, take that camp-stool, and sit down here where I can see you. Oh, dear me!" and Claude sighed wearily. " What red cheeks and what a brown skin you have, and how well and happy you look! How I envy you and such as you! You see I have all that money can buy, but not health and strength to enjoy it; and sometimes I think that I never shall be well, even if I live to be a man. But this is not what I meant to talk about. I've been thinking, since I spoke to

you the other day about those men, that
though they don't deserve any help, there
may be others who do, and I'm afraid we
have not thought as we should have done
of those whom we might assist. When my
mother was alive, I believe she used to visit
among the poor people in the town, and
wherever there was sickness or misfortune,
she was always ready to help and to comfort.
But since she has been gone, my father and
I don't seem to know what to do, or how to
do it, and indeed I fear we haven't thought
about it at all. Now it has occurred to me,
Charles, that you perhaps could tell me of
some good people who really need a little
help given in a quiet way. I positively get
tired thinking of myself, and what I wish,
and what I like, and I should enjoy trying
to do something for others for once."

And Claude smiled sadly, and fixed his
eyes on Charlie's bright face, with an un-
satisfied longing in them which the young
fisherman could not but notice.

"You're very good, sir," said Charlie, "to
take an interest in the poor folk. I think I
could tell you of some people as would never
ask for anything, indeed, as would rather

starve than beg, but finds it very hard, for all
that, to scrape along.   And if so be, sir, you'd
not be too proud to go yourself and see some
of them, and say a kind word to them now
and again, that would do them more good
than all beside, and there ain't one as wouldn't
be glad to see you."

"Really, do you think so?"

"Yes, sir, I don't even *think*, I am sure of
it.   Now there's old Widow Hagan.   She
lives on what the parish gives her, and the
parson helps her sometimes out of the poor
fund, but it's very hard for her to live.   She
knowed the lady at the Hall when she were
alive, and many a time when I've took her a
mackerel or a fresh herrin' (fish bein' about
all as ever *we* has to give) she's said to me,
'Oh, Charlie, how I miss that dear good lady,
Madam Rivington.   There ain't no one now
to say a kind word, or to come in and read
me a chapter out of the blessed book, when
my old eyes is dim and can't see to read it
to myself.'

"And then, sir, there's that poor little
cripple, Mat Sands, as lives with his step-
father; the man is good to him after his
fashion, but the child is a little delicate thing,

like a girl, and rough folks as we be doesn't understand how to manage them sort."

Just then Charlie was called away by the sailing-master to attend to some duty, and there was no more chance of talk that day. But this was the first of several conversations which took place between the two lads ; and gradually Charlie found himself becoming really attached to Claude Rivington, and he often wondered how he could ever have envied any one with so little pride, and so much kindness of heart.

One morning the *Sea Gull* was at anchor quietly in Wavebury Bay, John Walter was out fishing, and Charlie was at liberty. A few days previously Claude had expressed a wish to possess some of the pebbles and pieces of cornelian which were to be found on that coast, but which, owing to the many seekers during the summer and autumn months, were rare in the immediate neighbourhood. And this being a free day, Charlie resolved to employ it in walking over to a bay about six miles off; a lonely place where, in former times, he had found pebbles and cornelian, and even now and then bits of amber, washed up by the sea.

The tide was on the turn, beginning to go down, as Charlie started; so he knew he should arrive at the bay just at the best time to secure whatever the retreating waves might leave during the next few hours.

He took a bag with him, to hold any treasures that he might be fortunate enough to find, and his mother had packed up his dinner (consisting of a bloater, a small brown loaf and a bottle of cold tea) in a little basket which he slung by a strap round his waist. A hatchet stuck out of his pocket, for it was possible that he might have to break some of the stones, to see whether they were real agates or common pebbles.

Thus equipped, he set out on his six-mile walk, his plan being to go by the cliff, and return by the beach. At present the tide was still too high for him to pass the points of the different bays that formed the undulating coast line; but coming back, he calculated that the tide would be far out, and the walk would be a pleasant one over the sand, rocks, and shingle.

Charlie reached the bay without adventure of any kind, and there setting to work at once, he began to seek diligently, and was more successful even than he had expected to be. But after several hours of search, involving a constantly stooping posture in the full blaze of the sun, Charlie began to feel very tired, and when he had finished his dinner, he became so sleepy, that he thought he would try and find some cosy place where he could have a nap, and so be rested for his walk home. There was no fear of his over-sleeping himself, so as to be caught by the tide, for the water would be a long time in rising to the foot of the cliff, and in any case he could always return by the road instead of the shore. So he began to hunt about for some cosy little nook where he could lie down in the shade and rest for a while.

At last a pile of loose stones attracted his attention, and going behind it, he saw a rock placed rather curiously against the face of the cliff.

Somehow, to Charlie's observant and practised eye, the position of the rock did not look natural; not as if the waves had washed it to its place, or as if it had fallen there in a landslip. Taking hold of it, he put all his strength into trying to roll it on one side. With some little difficulty he succeeded, and was surprised to see that the rock had covered the entrance to a cave or grotto, such as is often found in the cliffs on the English and French coasts.

Of course there was nothing surprising in seeing a cave, for there were several of which Charlie knew between Wavebury and Turbot-town, the next town on the coast. But the strange part was that this cave should be so carefully concealed.

Stooping, the lad crept in, and found himself in a kind of grotto very much like the other caves that he had seen ; the sand under his feet was wet, showing that the water came in there at high tide, and scattered about were bits of shell and sea-weed, newly washed up.

"It may have been my fancy, after all," said Charlie to himself, "as that there rock had been put so by some one to hide the hole. Who'd care to hide anything, or to hide themselves in a place where they'd be drownded every high tide? And Charlie gave a little laugh, which sounded hollow and uncanny, as it left his lips, and made an echo in the curious, irregular roofing.

The broad daylight poured in through the

aperture by which Charlie had entered, and finding it too light to sleep, he managed, from the inside of the cave to draw the rock door towards him, until he had again closed the entrance, making it as it was before. Then he crept into a hidden corner, with the rough cliff wall on one side of him, a huge boulder on the other, and soft sand between.

The sound of the receding waves was in his ears, soothing him, like a mother's lullaby, to rest. His hot head rested on a pillow of cool sand ; his back and limbs, stiff and tired with stooping, were stretched at ease. What wonder then that the sense of comfort became drowsiness very soon ; the drowsiness a doze, and the doze a deep sleep, disturbed only by a strange dream, such a dream as Charlie had never had before.

CHAPTER III.

A DREAM AND A PLOT.

HARLIE WALTER dreamed that Claude Rivington and he were out in the *Sea Gull.* They were alone; no captain, no sailors; and the boat floated on as by magic, over smooth seas, out towards the west.

All of a sudden, up from some unknown hiding-place, appeared the grim faces and slouching forms of Black Darley and Crafty Joe. They approached the young Squire with menacing looks and gestures, and in his dream Charlie thought that he planted himself between the ruffians and Claude, to defend him; but even as he did so, a golden ship glided out into the sunset, and approached them, all sail set; and as it rapidly neared them, Charlie thought he saw a glorious form standing upon the deck; and with the gladness of recognition, a sense of safety, he said, " Lord, bid us come to Thee on the water." And over the shining sea, he thought a voice solemn and sweet as the note of an organ, came pealing in the one word, " Come!" And taking Claude's hand in his, the young fisher, without a fear, stepped down into the sea, and, lo, it was no longer water—no longer waves with blue depths and white crests, but a golden road, beautiful to look upon, and firm to the feet. And when he sought for the golden ship, lo, there was none, but in its place a glorious city, with high glittering walls and gates of pearl, and he knew that this must be heaven. But even as the rapturous thought filled his heart, the spell of the dream was broken, and he awoke, his feelings strangely divided between a sense of joy and the half consciousness of impending danger.

Charlie awoke, but he did not stir, for he heard two voices in earnest conversation, and as he listened, he became aware that the voices were those of Black Darley and Crafty Joe.

Concentrating all his energy in the effort to attend, he lay quite still, feeling rightly that much might depend upon his quick ears and self-possession, for it could hardly be that these two men were in this out-of-the-way place for any good purpose.

"Well," said Black Darley, " I shouldn't wonder if you was right, Joe; now's the time, if anything's to be done at all."

" Yes," replied the smoother but scarcely less unpleasant voice of Crafty Joe. " I met the Squire's groom as he were drinkin' at the Wavebury Arms t'other day, and when he'd had a few glasses, and began to feel jolly, I got out of him as how the Squire were expected next week; so there ain't over much time to spare. He told me, too, where the butler sleeps (it ain't with the silver, Darley), and lots more things what'll all come in useful."

" But you ain't a-goin' to keep nothin' to yourself, Master Joe, remember," growled Darley. " We go shares in this, or look out ! If you're the head in the thing, at least I'm the hands, and neither can't do nothin' without t'other."

" Now don't go for to put yourself in a

state," said Joe. "We can't neither of us do t'other much harm without doin' of it to ourselves too. And if that ain't a bond of union, I don't know one!" and the scoundrel laughed a low, oily laugh, which made the young listener shudder.

"Still," said Darley, "say that we take the silver, that's only robbin' the old Squire, and I should like to let the young one hev something to remember too. Such a stuck-up young jackanapes, ridin' and drivin' and sailin' round, as though he was the Emperor of Rooshy at least, when *we* has to walk with scarce a shoe to our feet."

"Well, there's a way in which we can spite him too," responded Joe. "The groom told me that the Squire's lady when she died left some family jewels—di'monds and such like—for her son, sayin' they was to be his wife's when he married. The groom heard all this from the under housemaid, what heard it from the upper housemaid, and she again had it from the lady's maid as used to be with the Squire's lady. And them jewels bein' his mother's as was, the young master sets great store by, and keeps in his dressin'-room. And to that there dressin'-room

c

winder there's a porch as faces the garden at the back of the hall, so nothin' could be more convenient, if they'd made it all on purpose. The Squire's lady, it seems, wouldn't hev the di'monds re-set in her day, cos she said it would be time enough for that when her son married; but I'm thinkin' we may as well save the jew'lers the trouble. I've a Jew friend as is goin' off to Holland next week, and he'll take the stones, and sell them for us, and the silver I can get melted down arterwards at Turbot-town."

"But till we get rid of it all, think you it will be safe to hide it here?" Black Darley said.

"Ay, safe enough," responded Joe; "I'd like to know who'd think of lookin' for silver and jewels in a cave at Agate Bay!"

"And yet folks does come here sometimes to look for stones," said Darley.

"Yes, but I don't believe no one but us has ever found out this cave; leastways, even if they did, they wouldn't guess there was a inner one, safe from the water, and big enough to put up a coach and six, if you could but drive them in."

At this, Charlie was so much astonished that he nearly made an exclamation, but checked himself in time.

"Well," said Joe presently, "when should you think was the best time to do our little affair at the Hall ? "

"To-night ? " suggested Darley.

" No, no, that's too soon. Say day after tomorrow, and it must not be earlier than one o'clock in the morning, 'cause some of the folks don't go to bed over and above early. But the Squire, they say, is the latest up when he's at home, so his bein' away gives us a better chance. I'll get the tools and instruments we want, so don't trouble your head about them; old Levi Abrams at Turbottown will lend me them; he's stood our friend more nor once, has old Levi, for he's up to the ways of folks. Talk of undertakers (that's his profession, you know), he's a undertaker more ways nor one. But it's gettin' late, Darley, and I've got to go on to Turbottown and get back afore night ; thank goodness, I han't got no missus at home to growl and grumble at me for not comin' in at the right time."

" But I hev, and worse luck to her," said

Black Darley, in a harsh voice that made the listener in the corner wince, and pity poor Mrs. Darley. "And I must get back as quick as I can. Have you a shillin' or two you can spare, Joe? I'll pay you back when we gets the swag."

"I've got sixpence I can let you hev, but no more; you must manage with that."

Darley took it with a sulky nod; then, after agreeing together which corner would be the best for the disposal of the treasure when it should become theirs, the two men left the cave, passing close by Charlie's hiding-place, while the boy held his breath, —his heart beating wildly with the dread of being discovered,—till he heard Crafty Joe scramble up the steep stony path to the cliff, then he listened to the soft, slow thud of Black Darley's great flat feet, taking the beach path homeward.

Charlie now stole from his corner, came to the entrance of the cave, and pushed aside the rock, which the men had replaced in the opening.

"I won't go home just yet," he said to himself; "I must have a look first at that inside cave; but perhaps I'd better just peep

out, and see that Black Darley's well away."
So saying, he leaned forward, bending on his
hands and knees, and peered cautiously out ;
and presently he saw the man clambering
over some rocks at the point that separated
Agate Bay from a rather longer, straighter
stretch of beach, which, from its smooth,
shining surface, went by the name of Silver
Sands.

In a moment more the man was fairly out
of sight, and Charlie turned back into the
cave, to explore this meeting-place of the
would-be burglars.

In search of the inner chamber of which
Darley and Joe had spoken, he went to the
very end of the cavern where he had fallen
asleep. There he observed what he had not
before noticed ; namely, a large round hole
partly hidden by a projecting boulder.

Through this hole he went without a
moment's hesitation, and found himself in
a spacious and perfectly dry place, lighted
dimly by what looked like cracks in the
irregular arch of the rocky roof, but carpeted
with the softest and most silvery sand, where
no wave ever washed, and of which the wind
never stirred one tiny grain.

Charlie paused in admiration. He had never seen such a wonderful place.

" I wonder if those fellows have got anything hidden here already, as well as what's to come!" said he, speaking aloud, as he had a habit of doing when absorbed in thought.

But, as the words left his lips, he felt himself suddenly seized from behind, and a voice hissed in his ear, " You young serpent, you meddlin', sneakin' wiper! what do you mean by bein' here, and by what you said? speak, or I'll —— " and the sentence ended in a dark look, as the face appeared dimly over Charlie's shoulder,—needing no words to make it sufficiently threatening,—and revealed to the lad that the man who had surprised him thus was no other than Crafty Joe.

CHAPTER IV.

A SWIM FOR LIBERTY.

OE SLIDE, after parting from Darley and walking for a short distance along the cliff towards Turbot-town, suddenly found that he had left behind him, in one of the cave's rocky corners, a bottle of gin, which he had that day bought, but which he had feared to keep about him while Darley and he were together, because he had no wish to share it with him. To regain his precious bottle, therefore, Crafty Joe had returned to the cave, found the outer rock moved aside, and had at once entered, secretly vowing vengeance against the intruder, whoever he might prove to be. Our readers may conclude, therefore, that the sight

of Charlie enraged him far more than that of
a stranger would have done, more especially
as the boy's words proved that in some way
he had become possessed of at least a part
of the secret. Besides, Joe had not forgiven
Charlie for his determined silence on the
subject of the Hall, when he and Darley had
endeavoured to draw him into conversation,
and to get from him some sort of informa-
tion.

With the heartiest good-will the ruffian
would have taken the boy's life then and
there, had he dared to do so. As it was,
he now remained undecided, wondering how
he might indulge his own evil passion for
revenge, and yet be safe from punishment.

At last, with a grin which distorted his
face out of all its usual hypocritical smooth-
ness, he said, loosening somewhat his tight
hold of Charlie's collar and arm,—

" Now, Charles Walter, you young sneak,
you've been and comed in here a-trespassin'
where you'd no business to come ; and you've
not been content with stayin' in t'other cave
even, but you must be pokin' that imperent
nose of your'n here beside ; but, as good
luck would have it, I've cotched you at your

little game. So now, my fine bird, you're a
prisoner, and you may just choose one of two
things. Either you promise me, faithful and
sure, as you'll help Darley and me in a job
we hev on hand in a day or two, or I'll fasten
you in here so as you won't get out in a hurry,
and you may starve for aught I care. Any
way I and Darley will do the job I spoke of
without you ; and if you can get out of this
cave, you'll only hev the pleasure of thinkin'
it's all over, and no gain to you neither. But
if you'll help us, askin' no questions now, we'll
treat you well, and give you your fair share
of all there is goin';" and here Joe's voice
changed again to something of its usual crafty
persuasiveness, which made Charlie shrink
with aversion as he had not yet shrunk with
fear.

"I know very well what you mean," replied Charlie, "and what job you want me
to join in ; and I tell you I'd rather stay
here and be starved to death than work with
you and Black Darley."

"Then if you knows what we're after,
young man," said Joe, dropping all his pre-
tence of softness and appearing once more
what he really was, "you're a dangerous

fellow to hev round loose. Still, I've heard
tell you can speak the truth, and I'll give
you one more chance. Say you'll not meddle
with our game (I ain't askin' you to join us
now), and you may go. Only if *then* you
dare to say a word about us, you'll repent it
for ever and a day."

A great temptation came to Charlie that
moment. Might he not promise, so as to
secure his freedom? He was not bound,
surely, to keep a promise extorted from him
thus, and if he escaped he could prevent
the robbery. But a moment's reflection convinced him that such reasoning was utterly
false, unmanly, and un-Christian, and that
God, who had permitted in His providence a
trial and danger like this to befall him, could
also, if it seemed good to Him, make a way
of escape for His child without his yielding
to what was wrong. So, taking courage from
this last thought, he answered firmly,—

"No, Joe; I'll give you no promise. I've
never told a lie yet, and I'm not goin' to
make a promise that I know I can't keep."

"Very well, then; you shall just stay here
till me and Darley makes up our minds
what we'll do. I'll go back to Wavebury

by-and-by ; and to-morrow, if folks takes to wonderin' why you're not home, I shall say I saw you in Agate Bay, as I were a-comin' home by the cliff, and that p'raps the tide cotched you as you was tryin' to get round the point."

Now Joe was crafty, and thought that the fear of causing his parents the sorrow of thinking he was lost or drowned would make Charlie give the required promise, which if once made he felt sure the lad would keep.

But Charlie had been thinking and praying silently, and had made up his mind that, come what might, he would not yield an inch to the tempter.

Besides, he felt almost certain that Joe would not dare to do anything very reckless or cruel, and was only threatening him to make him afraid. Charlie knew well enough that already this man and his companion in crime, Black Darley, bore the worst of characters in the neighbourhood, so that there was nothing now of which they could not be suspected. And who could tell what might be found out, and to what punishment it might lead ?

But, in addition to all this, a bright thought

had occurred to Charlie,—a way in which even yet he might escape from the clutches of his enemy, without giving too much anxiety to his parents by a very prolonged absence from home.

For the carrying out of his plan, however, it was necessary that he should keep on talking to Joe for some little time longer.

"I can't make you the promise you want, Joe ; so it's no use your speakin' of it," said Charlie, after a minute or two of quiet deliberation ; "but perhaps, now you've caught me, you'd like to know how I got here, and how I came to know what you and Black Darley was a-goin' to do."

"Yes!" replied Joe, with some appearance of curiosity, "you can sit down here and tell me while I take a dram. I'm tired with my walk and this confounded bother with you." So saying, he drew his bottle out of the dark corner, keeping, however, very close to Charlie, and fastening his watchful eyes upon him, even while he applied the fiery poison to his lips.

Drinking to excess was one among many of Crafty Joe's vices. Indeed, this evil habit was a perfect passion with him, potent and

irresistible. And when Charlie remarked
how the man's colour rose, and his eyes grew
bloodshot, as he swallowed eager gulps of
the coarse spirit, his hope of escape grew
almost to a certainty, especially when his
practised ear heard what Joe's duller per-
ceptions had not taken in; namely, the
quiet wash of the fast rising tide, which
had already stolen up to the entrance of
the outer cavern, was deepening there every
moment, and would soon be sending its
encroaching waters all over the cave that
Charlie had first entered.

Listening intently, but not showing that he
was doing so, Charlie, as leisurely as possible,
told the story of his expedition to Agate
Bay, of his sleep in the cave, and of his waking
to hear two men in conversation. He told
how he had watched Black Darley till he was
out of sight, and then how he had determined
to find out the inner cave ere his return home.
And as Charlie went on talking, Joe went on
drinking, till now there was only a little spirit
left in the bottle, while his eyelids began to
droop heavily, and, as if unable to support
himself, he leaned more and more over to
one side. He tried hard to keep himself

awake; he struggled against the drunken sleep that was creeping over him, but all to no purpose. A few minutes more, and he was sound asleep, snoring loudly; and Charlie, rising noiselessly, slipped off his boots and his jacket, and hid them in a corner, depositing there also his cap, his hatchet, his bag of stones, and his little dinner-basket. Then he stole on tip-toe to the hole that made the doorway between the two caves.

Yes—it was just as he thought; the body of the first cavern was full of water, or rather, judging from its depth by measuring with the eye the rocky walls, Charlie concluded that there were about four feet of water there already. The cave gradually shelved down towards the entrance on the beach, so that at the upper end (the one nearest the inner chamber) there was hardly more than a foot of water; nor could the tide rise so high as to get up to the second entrance, and thus flood the inner cave.

"Now for a wade and a swim!" thought Charlie. His plan was to wade through the water in the cave, shoot through the narrow entrance, and swim for a short distance, just far enough out to sea, to keep from being dashed against the rocks by the incoming tide. The water was very quiet to-day, so there was little or no surf; and by swimming for a few minutes he could get opposite to the cutting, up through the cliff. Just here, there was a little strip of smooth beach; and by suffering himself to come in on a wave of the fast flowing tide, he could gain a footing on the shore, and then go up the cutting to the cliff, and set off towards home. Nor was there any real danger in this plan to a lad who knew every inch of the coast, and who was as much at home in the sea as on land.

He stood looking for a moment at the quickly deepening water lying like a black pool in the dusk of the cave. Then he stepped in, and waded down towards the entrance, the water deepening at every step.

Here, putting his hands together, and stretching out his limbs in one vigorous stroke, he shot through the opening on a receding wave, and shook the drops from his face as he rose to the surface. Then, feeling the clear sky over him, and the generous sea lifting him up, he struck out on a line with the shore, so as to come opposite to the cutting.

Never before, in all his young life, had
Charlie felt such delight in his freedom, and
in his health and strength, as at this moment
of his escape; even as he swam with his
long, steady strokes, he could have shouted
for joy and exultation of spirit.

With a smooth, quiet roll, a wave, bearing
our young hero upon its breast, washed him
up on to the bit of beach, as easily as though
he had been one of those pink shells lying
about. And now, wringing the water from
his shirt and trousers, he began to climb the
cutting.

In a few moments he reached the top,
and pausing to recover breath, he turned and
looked out across the sea.

Again the sun was setting in gorgeous
beauty, and again, among the many vessels
that dotted the ocean far and near, one sailed
into the western glow, as on the day when
Charlie and his mother had watched the sunset together, and as it had appeared to him
in his dream this very afternoon.

"My golden ship again!" he murmured,
his whole face lighting up with pleasure.
Then, reminded of the feelings and thoughts
associated with the former occasions, and

full of thankfulness for to-day's experiences, the heart of the lad overflowed with grateful emotion, and there all alone on the cliff, he dropped on his knees, and poured out a prayer of thanksgiving and praise, consecrating himself afresh to the service of the Master who despised not the poor fishers of old, but loved them, and trusted them, and took them for His disciples.

It grew dusk as Charlie sped homeward, and glad enough he was of this, for though the road for the most part was very lonely, it was pleasant to think that the hatless, bootless, jacketless lad wending his way along the cliff, and looking very like a half-drowned tramp, would not be known as Charles Walter, as otherwise some curiosity might have been roused, and questions raised which would have been somewhat hard to answer.

As he walked briskly on in the deepening twilight towards Wavebury, the events of the day filled his thoughts.

How strangely all had come about! His discovery of the cave, his sleep there in a corner where he could not be seen ; his curious dream, his still stranger waking, and the disclosure of the plot against Claude Rivington

D

and the Hall. Then his being found by Crafty Joe while he was pursuing his investigations; and lastly his escape; the latter rendered as easy again as he had expected, by Joe's heavy, drunken sleep.

It had been Charlie's intention, knowing that Joe could not swim a stroke, to keep him in conversation, if possible, until the tide should be well up; and then, by a sudden spring, to get through the hole dividing the caves, and dash into the water, and so to the sea, where he felt sure that Joe could not follow him.

But, owing to Joe's helpless condition, Charlie had of course been able to act deliberately, and make good his escape without difficulty.

CHAPTER V.

LIFE LESSONS.

THE next morning, when Charlie came to open the cottage front windows before breakfast, whom should he see but Crafty Joe ? All the sliminess and all the ruffianism seemed, however, to have disappeared, and he looked woefully haggard and crestfallen. After a few hours of heavy sleep, he had waked up to a recollection of what had occurred, and as soon as the tide was low enough to permit his leaving the cave, he had come over to Wavebury, to entreat Charlie to say nothing about his discovery, assuring him that he and Darley, if they had ever *really* entertained the thought of robbing the Hall, should now certainly never think of it again.

Charlie had been having a long talk with

his parents overnight, and was glad that a proposition he then made had met with their entire approval.

"Joe," said the boy gravely "father and mother knows all that I know, for of course I told them as soon as I got home last night. But we none of us wants you and Darley to get into trouble, but rather that you might have a chance to start fair again, and try and earn a honest livin'. So father thought I'd better tell you as how if Darley and you gives up your plan, and tries to be straightforward and hard-workin' fishers, as you used, no one won't tell on you, and all will be right. But as you haven't earned nobody's trust yet, and it's right that the Hall and the young Squire should be protected, father's gone up there now, to speak to the butler and the housekeeper, and to advise them to move both silver and jewels to some safe place where no one can't get at them. You needn't be afeared, Joe," continued Charlie, seeing a look of real anxiety come over Joe's face; "father's not a-goin' to mention no names, but just to say that there had come to his ears a report as how the Hall might be robbed, seein' it were a

lonely place, and the Squire away; and so
he had come up to warn the head servants,
that things might be safe,—and recommend
them to hide the val'ables where no one
knowed but their two selves. So now, Joe,
you see the temptation to do this dreadful
thing is put out of your way, and if you'll
forgive me for speakin' so plain to you, won't
you be persuaded to take up your work again,
and give up drink, and be honest and happy?"

Joe did not reply at once. Charlie's face
was very earnest, his eyes were full of a kind
pitying light—the tones of his young voice
had in them an innocent persuasiveness. In
his face and manner and words there was no
trace of resentment for the harshness shown
him the day before; and Joe was somewhat
surprised at this.

"I don't know what to say to you, Charles
Walter, and that's the truth," said he, looking
down. "I must have a talk with Darley
afore I makes promises, and by the bye, how
did you get away last evening? When I
woke up you was nowhere, and all was pitch
dark, and the wind had got loose, and the
waves thunderin' up agen the cliff, and the
outer cave chock full of water."

Charlie gave him an account of his escape, which seemed to interest Joe not a little.

"I'll say this for yer, Charlie," remarked he, half unwillingly, as though the words were wrung out of him, in spite of conflicting feelings, "you're just the pluckiest lad that ever I see, and though you've diddled me and Darley as thorough as if you'd been a detective police officer in plain clothes, p'raps you've saved us in the long run, from a longer run still—over to Botany Bay, or somewheres else as nice. And after all, it were kind of yer not to mention names, but to give Blackie and I a chance of rightin' ourselves."

Now if there was one thing in the world for which Joe had an admiration, it was for what he called "*pluck.*" It was not among the gifts with which Heaven had blessed him, and perhaps for this reason Joe admired it the more. Goodness apart from it would never have impressed him; noble conduct and the truest generosity might have passed by unnoticed; but courage, both moral and physical, such as the lad had shown, appealed to the one side of his character which had not become utterly hardened to all that was beautiful and true. And now, for the sake of Charlie's pluck, Joe even consented to see his kindness and forgiving nature, and allowed himself to soften somewhat for the moment, though he took himself to task for his weakness, as he called it, as soon as he turned away.

What passed between Black Darley and Joe that morning was never known, but, a few days after, the fishermen were astonished to see these two usually idle fellows pushing off the old boat (now freshly repaired and well tarred) that used to carry them, and going out to sea.

The first free time that Charlie could get was spent in another visit to Agate Bay, to fetch his clothes, the bag of stones, his basket and hatchet, which had been hidden away in the inner cavern.

This time he met with no adventure; but got back to Wavebury by the shore before the tide rose, taking his bag of stones to the Hall, where they were gladly received by Claude.

The weeks passed swiftly, and with the frequent opportunities for intercourse afforded by the expeditions in the *Sea Gull*, it was not wonderful that these two lads, though so widely separated by their respective stations in life, and by the difference in their education and training, should feel their mutual interest deepening.

Indeed, by degrees a real friendship was springing up between them, and each found much to like and to admire in the other.

Claude was learning both to respect and to trust the brave, honest, manly fisher boy who yet had a heart tender as a child's, a strong sense of right and wrong, and a reverent feeling of dependence upon God's good Spirit, without whom he knew that his best efforts were in vain. And Charlie, on his side, looked upon his gentle, delicate, fair-haired young master with a respectful and loving compassion, a tender admiration; and while acknowledging his superiority in book-learning, and in the refinements of life, felt that he needed, in some sort, both guidance and protection.

Claude had taken Charlie's advice, and instead of driving or riding about aimlessly along the country roads, he had paid visits to many of his father's more distant tenants, and had rejoiced the hearts of some of the old people who had loved his mother in years that were gone, by chatting kindly and pleasantly with them. And little by little, as he saw how these poor folks lived— how contented they were, for the most part, with their hard lot, how thankful for a little unlooked-for brightness in their sky—a drop of unexpected sweetness in their cup—his thoughts and feelings underwent a change. He began to contrast his position with theirs, and to feel how selfish and self-indulgent he had hitherto been, how forgetful of others, and thus wholly unconscious of the joy that comes from being of use, and from having a work and a purpose in life.

Claude, since his mother's death, had left off reading his Bible, but now, since his talks with Charlie often turned upon passages of Scripture, and incidents from sacred history, and from the life of our Lord, he began to study, with renewed pleasure and interest, the New Testament especially. What he had learned as a child returned to him with fresh power, and, sincerely repenting of his past coldness and carelessness, and trusting for forgiveness and acceptance through the finished work of the Saviour, to whom his heart had been drawn, Claude Rivington began to see life from a different aspect; and his intercourse with Charlie, whose Christianity was of a simple and practical kind, was helpful to Claude, and corrected his somewhat indolent and dreamy tendencies. Charlie had always taken an especial interest in the life of the disciple Peter. His fisherman's calling, his warm, impulsive nature, his ardent love for the Saviour, his great sin and bitter repentance ; and the strange mixture of faith and unbelief, of physical courage and moral cowardice, of strength and weakness, that formed part of his earlier character—and the nobleness, the Christian boldness, the self-forgetfulness, the faith of his later years, all these had taken hold of Charlie's sympathies, ·and made him wish sometimes that he could have lived in the days when Christ was on earth, so that he also might have been among the disciples, and have followed the Lord whithersoever He went.

And Claude too caught the warmth and the enthusiasm that made the New Testament history such a reality to Charlie.

He too began to see that Christ's presence in the every-day life, its joys, its works, its amusements, gave vitality and brightness and beauty. He too began to hear the Saviour's voice saying, "Follow Me," and his heart responded to the call of the Divine Master.

In one of the long conversations between the lads, Charlie had told Claude about his dream in the cave (though not of the adventure that succeeded it, or that there was a second cave in the inner portion of the cliff), and Claude had smiled a quiet, happy smile at the beautiful ending of the dream, and said, "Oh, Charlie, it may come true after all; you may be the one to lead me to heaven, just as you dreamed that you and I went hand in hand along the shining road across the sea. I did not care for these things before, but now I am beginning to love them; and I shall never see your golden ship in the sun-lit ocean, without thinking of what you have told me."

Autumn had come; the busiest fishing-time of the whole year, and just now John Walter was unfortunately laid up with rheumatism, and could not even turn in bed, much less go out fishing; so upon Charlie devolved the work which was to support the family. And hard work it was, for the weather was more than usually bad, and often the storm-signals were hoisted, and not a boat could put out to sea, or else having started, Charlie would have to come toiling home against wind and tide, with little or no fish to show for his day's work.

In spite of the little savings of years, which now stood them in good stead, it would have been hard to live, had it not been for the kindness of Claude Rivington. He paid daily visits to the old man's cottage, bringing him delicate food, paying for his doctor's visits, and for the necessary medicines; reading to him out of the Bible all the fisherman's favourite chapters, and comforting and cheering both John and his wife, until they told him—much to his delight—that he was every day growing more and more like "that sainted lady," his mother.

The first little airing that John took was in Claude's pony carriage, driven by the young Squire himself; and never did purer joy fill Claude's heart than when the old man—set down refreshed and invigorated at his own door—turned to him and said,—

" God bless and reward you, sir—God bless you for all you've done for me ; and——" here he uncovered his grey head, and looked up solemnly, adding, "and, sir, He will—He will."

CHAPTER VI.

THE PRISONERS OF THE CAVE.

EPTEMBER went by, and with it passed the equinoctial gales, and October, with its chill nights but bright, brisk days, had come. A glorious time was this at the sea-side, and the Hall was merry with young voices, and the sound of young feet, for a number of Claude's cousins had come to spend a month with him, and greatly they were enjoying themselves.

Charlie Walter of course saw less of the young Squire than formerly, but this was no one's fault, and Charlie was busy enough not to miss his friend, as he might otherwise have done. The sailor whose place Charlie had filled on board the *Sea Gull* was well again, and had returned to his work, and oftener than ever now the pretty yacht spread her snowy wings and danced over the waves, bearing the happy party from the Hall. And on the days when the sea was a little too rough for pleasure-sailing, all the horses from the Hall stables were in requisition, and some of the party driving, some riding, they would go long distances, generally taking their luncheon with them, and returning home in the evening, noisier and merrier and happier than ever.

One morning, about ten o'clock, Charlie, who had been to the Hall with fish, saw Claude and his cousins setting out for a drive. Claude stopped the pony-chaise, while the wagonette and mail-phaeton went on.

"Good morning, Charlie," said he; "we are going for a picnic to Agate Bay. My cousins want to find some stones to take home and have polished, and I mean to try and find out your cave if I can." Then, before Charlie could reply, Claude drove off.

The young fisherman called out after him, "Look out for the tide, sir; it will be high about five o'clock!" But whether Claude heard him or not Charlie could not be certain; for the young Squire only turned his head and nodded, and that might have meant anything or nothing.

John Walter's smaller boat (for he had two) wanted a coat of paint to keep the wood sound, and as John himself was obliged to be out fishing all that day and night, he had charged Charlie to see to the painting. The lad, he knew, could turn his hand to anything, and would do the job as well as any painter in Wavebury or Turbot-town. So Charlie set to work on the beach by the little pier; singing blithely as a bird, and now and then lifting his head, to see the bathers nearer the centre of the bay's deep curve, or the fishing-smacks and pleasure boats out at sea, looking like big birds gliding along, dipping their breasts in the sparkling blue-green of the water.

Charlie worked hard all the morning, going home to dinner at one o'clock, then back to the boat in the afternoon. At three o'clock he had finished, and the boat was drying nicely in the brisk salt wind that blew straight from the sea.

When he reached home, he was surprised to see there the Squire's groom.

"You're just in time, Charlie," said Mrs. Walter, "to answer a question from the Hall. The Squire's out, but the housekeeper have sent over to know if, while you was on the beach, you've seen any of the young ladies or gents. They sent the carriages home this mornin' from Agate Bay, meanin' to return on foot by the sands."

"No," replied Charlie; "I haven't seen nothin' of any of them, and if they wanted to come by the beach they ought to be home directly now, for it'll be high tide in a couple of hours or less; but there oughtn't to be any danger," he added, after a moment's thought; "for there's a cuttin' up through the cliff right in Agate Bay itself, so they can come home that way. If only they haven't started rather late for home, and got caught at any point on the shore, they're safe enough."

Still, the lad could not shake off a feeling of uneasiness, though the groom looked relieved, and said he should carry the message back to the Hall. While Mrs. Walter added that her Charlie's word about tides was equal to any one's, for he knew all about them as well as his father did," and that apparently was the highest praise that the good woman could bestow.

When the man was gone, Charlie turned to his mother and said, "I think, mother, I'll just walk on towards Agate Bay by the cliff; the path runs along by the edge for the most part of the way, and if I should see any of them coming home by the sands, I could show them where they could get up the cliff, if the water was high. The wind's blowing fresh, and will bring the tide up more than usual to-day."

So saying, Charlie set off at a brisk run along the cliff, keeping close by the edge, so as not to miss any signs of the young people of whom he was in search.

The tide was rising rapidly, and he could not help hoping that Claude and his companions, seeing this, had decided to return by the cliff, in which case he should meet them.

In this expectation, he went quickly along, sometimes at a walk, but more often at a run, until the whole of the distance was traversed, and he stood at the top of the cutting above Agate Bay.

E

The water covered the beach right up to the cliff, and there were no signs of any living creature near. Charlie felt sure he had not missed them on his way there, so they had clearly not returned either by the shore or the cliff. There was but one place where they could be, and at this sudden thought which struck him, Charlie threw off boots, jacket and cap more quickly if possible than he had done on the memorable afternoon of his escape from Crafty Joe.

"They are in that cave!" he said to himself, "and the tide has caught them there, and they can't get away, and they don't know about the inner one, for I didn't tell the young Squire anything of the story but just the dream. Half an hour more, and it might be all up with them!"

Another moment, and having reached the base of the cliff where his feet touched the water, he made a few steps forward, then began to swim against the tide with bold, strong strokes till he could get just opposite the cave. Making the entrance, however, was a far more difficult thing than escape from the cave had been on the former occasion. The sea was rougher now, the tide was higher, and Charlie knew that there was danger of his been carried up on a wave and dashed against the rocks above the cave's mouth, while he was trying to find his way inside.

To avoid this, he let himself float on the wave, only a certain distance. Then, before it broke, he dived, and thus shot head first into the cave.

Coming in from the light, he could see nothing at first, but a glad cry greeted him, and in a few seconds—during which his eyes became accustomed to the darkness—he saw the frightened group of young people, crowded all together at the upper end of the cavern, up to their waists in water already, and evidently expecting nothing but death, and that very shortly. Claude was the only calm one.

"Dear, faithful Charlie," said he, "how did you know we were here? But it's no use; we cannot swim as you can, and the tide is rising still. We must be drowned."

"No, sir, you mustn't, and please God you won't neither," replied Charlie. "This is what I came to say. Just move a step, sir, please, can you? There—do you see this rock high up here behind you ? At the back of it there's a big hole, and if you'll please to get through, you'll find yourself in a safe, dry place; and if all the young gentlemen and ladies will do the same, I'll go back the way I came, and tell them as is anxious about you that you're all right."

One by one the girls and boys scrambled through the opening, Claude last; and Charlie, as he stood there, heard their exclamations of delight and thankfulness. But Claude looked down at him through the rocky doorway, and said sadly, " Oh, Charlie, Charlie, again you are risking your life. Stay here—*do* stay. See, the cave is nearly full of water now ; it is over your shoulders as you stand, you will be drowned."

" No, sir, no," replied the young fisherman cheerily. " I've done it before, and I think I can manage it again. The Squire would be terrible uneasy about you, sir, if you wasn't to come home, and he was to hear nothin' of you neither. Good-bye, Mr. Claude, don't be so anxious ; the good Lord takes care of us all. You'll see me again, or hear from me afore very long, please God."

A SWIM FOR LIFE.

And then the young Squire gave a gasp and a cry, for Charlie dived into the very centre of the dark pool, and shot through the opening without Claude catching sight of him again.

Nothing but the boy's long practice in swimming, and his dexterity sometimes in dodging the waves, sometimes in making use of them, could (humanly speaking) have saved Charlie Walter's life that afternoon. Again and again, ere he could reach the foot of the cutting, he was nearly swept against the great rocks that made a natural breakwater here and there; and to be dashed against them meant death! But the lad's coolness and presence of mind never forsook him, though his strength was well nigh spent when he scrambled up out of the water, and tried to climb the steep, stony pathway. Indeed, he was obliged to sit down for a few minutes, and recover his breath and strength, for his limbs gave way under him, and he was panting heavily. But he was soon rested, and picking up his outer garments, he started for Wavebury at a brisk, steady pace.

Quick as he was, however, before Charlie reached the Hall the Squire had returned home, and finding that the young people had not yet come in, he had grown very anxious, and was on the point of sending out servants in various directions to inquire and look for the young wanderers, while he himself prepared to go along the cliff, accompanied by Claude's mastiff, whose instinct, he hoped, might lead him in the right direction.

It was just at this moment that Charlie made his appearance, and meeting Mr. Rivington at the Hall gates, told him the whole story, and set his mind at rest.

"The tide won't be very long, sir, before it gets low enough to let them come out of the cave," added Charlie; "it's past the turn now; and if, sir, you can send the carriages by the cliff road to meet them, when they mount the cuttin' at Agate Bay, they would get home nice and quick. And if I might make so bold as propose such a thing, sir, I'd ask if you'd allow me to go with one of the carriages, as there may be ways in which I can help the young ladies and gentlemen, seein' as how I know the place so well."

"Nay, my lad," replied the Squire, laying a hand on Charlie's shoulder, "it's few requests of yours I could refuse to-night, and, after all, this is nothing for yourself, but all for us. My son is full of your praises, Charles Walter, and I am convinced now that he was right in his opinion of you. But come into the house, my lad, and have your clothes dried a bit, and drink a cup of hot coffee to warm you, unless you will have brandy and water ; but, now I think of it, you and your parents are teetotalers, are you not? And really, Charles Walter, you do credit to the principles of total abstainers.

" But come ; after such an exploit as yours (for though you make nothing of it, I am not blind either to its difficulties or dangers), you must need some rest and refreshment, and, according to your own showing, if the carriages were to set off at once, they would still have to wait some time on the cliff above Agate Bay before the tide was low enough to admit of our young people leaving the cave ; so there is no hurry. Thank God, my son and the rest are safe. Bless you, Charles, no one else could have done what you have done this day for me and mine, and I shall never forget it—never !" And the Squire took Charlie's rough brown hand in his, and wrung it hard, and the lad saw that there were tears in the eyes that he had always thought so proud and cold.

So Charlie sat by the fire in the house-keeper's room, dried his clothes, and drank hot coffee, till he felt warmed right through, and strong enough to have done his after-noon's work over again, had it been neces-sary.

When it was time for the carriages to start for Agate Bay, the Squire insisted upon Charlie's taking a seat beside him in his own special phaeton, while the big wagonette followed, carrying plenty of warm wraps to fold around the wet, chilled young folks, and a bottle of spicy cordial, to bring them warmth and comfort, after the exposure and terrible nerve strain.

When the carriages reached the cliff above Agate Bay, the tide was not yet quite low enough for the prisoners to make their exit with perfect safety; but in less than half an hour Charlie went down to the beach, waded round the rocks, and entered the cave; and presently out he came again, followed by the whole party of liberated prisoners, pale, shivering, but most glad and grateful for their deliverance.

Oh, what joy was at the Hall that night, and not less in the fisherman's cottage at Wavebury; for old John Walter and his wife could not but be proud of their brave Charlie, and he was very happy and thankful to have been able to render a real service to his dear Mr. Claude, and to Squire Rivington, towards whom Charlie's heart had warmed not a little that day.

Claude was quite ill for about a week after the memorable occasion we have just recorded. The immersion for so long in cold water, and still more the shock to a delicate system, brought on an acute attack of the chronic disorder from which he suffered, and for some days he could not leave his bed.

He would have liked, during this time of confinement to the house, to have seen much of Charlie, but the young fisherman was now at his busiest, for old John was still rheumatic and feeble, and the greater part of the more trying duties fell to Charlie's share. Indeed, it was evident enough that John Walter would very shortly be obliged to give up getting his living on the sea, and often he and his wife talked over their possible future, and sighed at the thought of being a burden upon their son, though they knew very well that he would never regard them as such.

Anyway, just now the state of John's health kept Charlie fully employed, and it was but seldom that he could run up to the Hall, sometimes carrying some dainty fish that he had caught, and which he thought the young Squire might fancy for supper or breakfast; sometimes bringing a rare shell or a pretty stone picked up on the beach, or found in the net while fishing. And these meetings were a great pleasure to the two lads. Now and then each would take a Bible, and there would be a sober, earnest talk on the meaning of certain passages; occasionally, as Claude got better, he would give Charlie a lesson in arithmetic or dictation, for the time of which we are writing was long before the establishment of compulsory education, and the young fisherman's learning (except so far as he had taught himself by reading his Bible, by quiet thought, and by habits of observation) had been very imperfect.

It would have been difficult to say which of the two boys enjoyed these lessons most, master or pupil, for to both they were a genuine satisfaction. They only regretted that they could meet so seldom.

"Charlie," said Claude one day, after one of these rare and richly-prized lessons, "what has become of those two men whom I saw a good time ago, on the cliff? I did not know their names, if you remember, and you told me who they were. They looked at me that day as if they hated me, and that made me think of them again and recollect them. Darley and Slide, I think you called them, did you not?"

"Yes, sir; Black Darley and Crafty Joe is the names they go by in the village. A little while ago, we hoped that they was turnin' industrious and honest, for I see them out fishin' pretty reg'lar, but after a bit they gave that up, and now I hear Crafty Joe's emigrated to America; and how Black Darley will get on without his mate, I don't know, for no one else will have anything to do with him, and they say the boat as belonged to both of them is sold, and of course Joe's took half the money to help him on his way, and Darley 'll soon drink up his half. I do pity his wife, Mr. Claude; if ever a woman were hardly used, it's that poor Mrs. Darley. Perhaps you'll scarcely believe it, sir, but I've seen that good, kind, patient creature when her eyes was red and green and yellow and blue, for all the world like some queer, sad rainbow, as hasn't got any hope or promise in it—and all from blows of that man's heavy hand. He's none too gentle when he's sober, but he's a wild beast when he's drunk, and that's not seldom, I'm afeared."

"I wonder if he has always been like this," said Claude; "or whether it is only of late years that he has become so."

"I believe, sir, that he used to be altogether different. Father says that he knew him as quite a young chap, and then there was no harm in him, save that he was a bit idle now and again. But he got in with bad companions, and learned drinkin' from them, and all sorts of wickedness, and since then he's gone down the hill—so to speak; but father says it's the drink as began it."

"It seems to me to begin so many things," replied Claude thoughtfully. And, dear readers, Claude Rivington was right.

CHAPTER VII.

CHAMPION TO THE RESCUE.

UTUMN had gone by, and winter had come. At least winter in its first stages; cold winds and cold rain, and bare brown fields, and now and then a frosty night and a bitter fog.

John Walter was again laid up with rheumatism, and once more Charlie was the bread-winner of the family.

He need not have worked so hard, for Claude was always trying to help, and urged Charlie to let him do more; but though the young fisherman deeply felt his friend's kindness, and accepted it gratefully, so far as help for his sick father was concerned, he was of far too proud and independent a nature to look to any one but himself for his mother's or his own daily bread. And Claude admired the lad's manly spirit, and yielded the more readily because Mr. Rivington and he were preparing something for the Walter family, which would be ready before very long, and would relieve John and his wife of all anxieties as to the future, and Charlie of the hard and incessant toil necessary now for the support of the family. But we are, we fear, showing that authors are bad hands at keeping a secret, so we will not let the cat out of the bag any further, but wait for the right moment to tell the pleasant little plot which had been hatching at the Hall since that eventful afternoon at Agate Bay.

Claude Rivington was riding home one night on his favourite mare, Lady Clare, and accompanied only by his mastiff, Champion. The dog had attached himself to his young master, and of late had gone with him whenever he walked or drove out. A magnificent animal was Champion, with his massive head, wide chest, intelligent face, and grave, earnest eyes ; quiet and good-natured enough too, but then he never was provoked or irritated, so that his temper had not yet been tried.

Had he been as savage as he was powerful, a wolf would have proved a far less
dangerous enemy than Champion.

On two occasions only, since Claude had
been his master, had the dog seemed to throw
off his accustomed dignified composure, and
show that he could feel resentment, or, at
least, a righteous indignation and strong
sense of justice.

One of these occasions was when, as
Claude was driving out one afternoon, he
suddenly, on a turn in the road, spied,
through a low gate that led into a field, a big
boy beating a smaller one unmercifully. The
little fellow was crying out loudly; but before
Claude had time to jump out of the chaise
and secure the ponies, Champion bounded
across the road, sprang, with wonderful agility
for so large a dog, over the fence, and collaring
the cowardly bully, threw him down and stood
growling over him, as though he were scolding
him well for his ruffianly conduct.

At first Claude was alarmed, for he knew
that the bite of so large a dog would be
dangerous. But as he came forward he found
that Champion had not attempted to bite the
lad, but had only grasped his collar with his

F

teeth, shaken the young miscreant, as he well deserved, and thrown him down. The noble beast came away quietly enough when Claude, after a few words to the boy, called Champion to follow him ; but it was evident now that the dog was neither lazy nor lethargic, nor even indifferent to what was going on around him.

Another occasion on which Champion showed himself capable of being thoroughly roused, was one morning, only a fortnight previous to the evening ride of which we shall presently tell.

As Claude was walking, with his dog, through the principal street of Wavebury, they came upon two or three curs worrying a poor cat, set on by a number of bad boys, who thought it fun to watch poor pussy's terror, and her brave, though feeble, efforts to defend herself.

Claude, determining to interfere, walked forward towards the group. But Champion was too quick for him ; with a great bound he dashed right into the middle of the discomfited band, gave one dog a shake which made it howl for ten minutes, and showed his teeth so savagely at the boys that they took

AN UNEXPECTED DEFEAT.

83

to their heels and fled ignominiously. Only poor puss lay there, panting and exhausted, and could not move a step. But Champion took her up softly, by the nape of the neck, in his great jaws, walked slowly with her to the opposite side of the street and placed her gently on the sidewalk, then trotted back to his master and looked up in his face, wagging his tail and saying as plainly as words could have said, " Now, haven't I been a good doggie ? Haven't I been a succourer of the oppressed, and a punisher of the evil-doer ? Pat me, dear master, for I really think I deserve it."

But to resume. It so happened that on this particular evening Claude had stayed out later than usual, and a cold fog was creeping up from the sea, adding to the darkness of night, and to the chill feeling in the air. Indeed, so dark was it that Claude, before he reached the cliff path, drew up the Lady Clare to a walk, as he could not see the road before him with any distinctness, and feared some accident if he rode too quickly.

But as he passed a little copse, or rather plantation, which lay to the right of the road, a figure suddenly started out from the shelter of the young trees and brushwood, and caught hold of the horse's bridle with one hand, and of Claude's arm with the other, while a deep harsh voice said, " Now, sir, quick; your purse and your watch, or it 'll be the wuss for you ! "

Claude touched his mare with the spur, and she made a bound forward, but the bridle was held too firmly for her to get away. Her movement, however, served to free Claude's right arm from the grasp of the would-be highwayman, and, though loth enough to strike, he raised the butt end of his whip, and let it descend heavily upon the hand that held Lady Clare's rein. At the same moment, with a savage growl which had a terrible sound even to Claude's ears, Champion, who till now had been trotting quietly behind at some distance, sprang upon the ruffian, and tore him down. Uttering a cry of mingled rage and fear, and a horrible oath, the man aimed a blow at the animal's face with his clenched fist, and in return the dog, who hitherto had not bitten him, made his great sharp teeth meet in the fleshy part of his shoulder. Claude threw himself from his horse, and knelt down by his fallen foe, making Champion drop his hold. The man's face was muffled up, and his head drooped forward, while the wounded shoulder, with its torn coat-sleeve, was uppermost as he lay on his side. Even when the dog let go of his shoulder he did not move, perhaps fearing another attack.

At last Claude said : " I hope you are not so much hurt but that you can get up and go home, if you have a home. I am sorry my dog has bitten you, but you know it was his duty to defend me ; and even after he had thrown you down he would not have hurt you, had you not struck him. Tell me the truth, now. What made you stop me to-night ? You must have been desperate indeed, if this was your only chance of getting money."

The man replied only by a surly grunt, which was answered by Champion, who growled threateningly.

" If you have been in trouble," continued Claude gently, laying a hand on Champion's great head to keep him quiet, " if you have been in trouble and poverty, I can feel for you, and can the more easily forgive you. Will you tell me your name, and where you live ? "

" No, I won't," replied the man savagely.

" Then you put it out of my power to help you," replied Claude. " And yet," he added, "your voice is familiar to me, and though I cannot see your face, I could almost fancy that the name you go by here is that of Black Darley. Now, am I right ? "

The man sprang to his feet with another horrible oath, which ended in a groan, for in his sudden movement he had lifted his shoulder, and the pain was intense.

Claude laid his hand on the man's arm, saying quietly, and in a clear, refined voice which made every word distinct and forcible : " I *am* right then ? Listen, Darley; though I know you, I do not mean to take advantage of my knowledge in the way you may think. Go home now, and fear nothing. I will send you a doctor from Turbot-town to attend to your shoulder. He is less likely to talk about this affair than a Wavebury surgeon. Meanwhile have the wound well bathed with hot water. Now go home, before it gets more stiff and painful."

There was no reply to Claude's kind, generous words. Whatever evil spirit of envy, discontent, and covetousness had driven

Black Darley to this guilty and dangerous attempt to get money, it had not gone out of him yet.

Not a word of thanks, not an expression of repentance escaped him; with another grunt he turned away and vanished in the mist, while Claude remounted, and, finding his way back into the regular high road, trotted briskly off towards Turbot-town. He felt sure that the man would go home. What he had said to him would have prevented his trying to escape, even had he been less severely bitten. And Claude wanted to see the doctor himself before sending him to Darley's cottage, to tell him the story, and ensure his silence upon the subject.

In nothing, perhaps, had the change in Claude's character been so marked as in the gentleness and tenderness he showed towards others.

Becoming gradually aware of the selfish life he had been leading, of his utter unmindfulness of the wants and needs of others, and of his care—in a lazy, languid way—only for his own comfort and pleasure, he had compared his life and character with that of his mother, whose memory so many treasured to this day.

Then, too, Charlie's advice about the poor folks had been thankfully followed, and thus, as Claude's eyes were opened, as a deeper sense of Divine love filled his heart, that heart grew very soft and tender towards the faults and weaknesses, as well as the sufferings, of his fellows, and he was far more ready than he had formerly been to make allowances and to forgive ; partly because he felt how much had, through Christ, been forgiven him, and partly because his experience and observation had now taught him that people's poverty and misery often tempt them to wickedness, and that love and kindness, in such cases, were the best means of reform ; a power which God Himself bids us use in His name for the reclaiming of the wanderer, and for pointing him to the Great Source of Love, a dying and risen Lord, through whom alone is salvation and sanctification.

Full of pity, therefore, and hoping that he might yet, perhaps, by God's help win poor Black Darley back to the right way, Claude Rivington rode briskly on, nor drew rein until he reached Dr. Wharton's door.

CHAPTER VIII.

MORE ABOUT BLACK DARLEY.

Lack Darley lay at home ill in bed, waited upon by the wife whom he had ill-used, and whose heart he had well-nigh broken; supported by the young Squire whom he had tried to rob; and visited by Charlie Walter whom he had cordially hated as "an obstinate jackanapes, and a meddling marplot."

If ever "coals of fire" burnt, then should they burn now, for never were they heaped with more generous hands than those which at this time helped and tended Black Darley.

Champion's bite, however well deserved, had been a terrible one, and the man's intemperate habits, and hot, uncontrolled temper, had retarded the healing process, so that fever had come on, and erysipelas, which had spread all over the arm, shoulder and neck, now threatened the head. And the devoted wife nursed the patient day and night with unwearied tenderness, though he never returned a word of thanks. And Dr. Wharton drove over from Turbot-town daily, his able services bespoken and amply recompensed by Claude Rivington, whose kindness was not even acknowledged by the sick man; while Charlie's visits were rewarded generally by a scowl or a surly grunt.

"We are making no progress with him, Charlie," said Claude one day, when, after half an hour spent at Darley's bedside, he met Charlie on his way home. "His shoulder is healing at last, but his heart is as stubborn and as hard as ever. I have done all I can; I have been as gentle with him as I know how; as far as may be I have shielded him from the consequences of his sin against me, and yet all seems useless. Only to-day I thought perhaps, that as he had been quieter than usual, he would let me read a few words to him out of my little Testament; and I said, 'Darley, may I read you a verse or two about some One who loved the world so much as to die for it, and who cured sick people and blessed little children?' And only think, Charlie. Scarcely had the words left my lips when he said roughly, 'No, sir, none of them Boibly books for me! I can't a-bear them!'"

"Did you ever try *tellin'* him a story, sir?" asked Charlie, after a moment's thought. "Maybe he'd listen to what you *told* him, even when he wouldn't let you read. He's been a fisher in his time, and a sailor too. Tell him, sir, as *you* can—that story out of the fourteenth of Matthew as was always such a comfort and pleasure to me, ever since I could understand anything. Tell him, sir, about the ship on the water, and the disciples toilin' and rowin' with the wind against them; and then about Jesus walkin' on the water, and Peter wantin' to go to Him, and tryin' it for a bit, and then beginnin' to sink, and cryin' 'Lord, save me!' That's a story as can't but take right hold on him, and if you can get him to listen once, sir, he'll do it again; and meanwhile, sir, we can pray for him—you and me—there's nought too hard for the Lord, and He can make this poor fellow's heart as soft as a child's." And Claude, taking courage and feeling hopeful once more, pressed Charlie's hand cordially, and the two lads parted.

No one but Mrs. Darley, Charlie Walter, and the doctor had been told of Claude's adventure, or how Darley's illness had been brought on. It had been carefully kept from the neighbours, because Claude was anxious to give the man one more chance for turning honest and respectable, and had people only guessed what Darley had tried to do, he could never have shown his face among them again. And Charlie, who had been the means of discovering and putting a stop to the first plot in which Black Darley had been concerned, felt that if ever the man was to be reclaimed, it must be now; and he heartily sympathized with the young Squire, who showed so sweet and forgiving a spirit, and was so anxious to benefit the patient—body and soul.

Darley would always speak more freely with Charlie than with Claude, probably because he disliked him less; since it seems a rule of nature that we must hate people whom we envy, and that this hatred grows in proportion to the license we give it, and to the harm we try to work to the objects of our envious feeling.

One evening, when Charlie had brought Black Darley a fine mackerel (which he himself had caught), and was sitting by the sick man's bed while Mrs. Darley broiled the fish for her husband's supper, some reference was made to Crafty Joe, from whom a letter had recently come from Canada, saying that he had found work, and was trying to make an honest living.

"A honest livin'!" repeated Darley; "well, p'raps he may out there, where no one knows him, and he can get good work and good pay. But tain't so easy for any one here, sitiwated like me. Here it's live by your wits, or starve. And talkin' of that, what a fine trick you played us—me and Joe— Master Charles Walter! Bless me if I couldn't have wrung your neck like a chicken when Joe told me the story! You're a mar-plot, and no mistake. Seems as if nothin' I try to do ever gets on. Fishin' didn't bring me in enough to live on (if you counts the gin as is needed to keep out cold and wet), smugglin's too risky, and it's oncertain beside. Then we see other folks rollin' in riches, and says I to myself and Joe, 'Why shouldn't we have some of that?' But no, though me and Joe finds

a place for consultin' in and for hidin' what
we might get—though we finds a place, I say,
what no one else has ever found, for all we
know—there must needs be a listener and a
spy, and that was you. And even when Joe
catches you, you manage to get away, while
the tide keeps him till next day. And then
when Joe goes off to Canada and I'm left to
myself, I says, says I, 'Now, if I could just get
one good lump of money at a time, I'd cut
away across the sea, and follow Joe;' and I
thought I'd leave my old missus behind, and
begin all over again alone. And once more
I says to myself, ' Look here, Darley, there's
that young Squire as has everything in the
world, though he be but a lad ; and here's
you as has nothin', and you a grown man, and
gettin' on in years, if in nought else. You
might as well take some of what he's got to
spare ;' and that's what I tried to do. But
that dog sets upon me like a wild beast, and
again I didn't get what I set my heart on."

"But it really was envy that made you
want to do both those things, now wasn't it,
Darley ?" asked Charlie.

"Well, yes, I s'pose so," replied the man.
" You see, it seemed sort of hard that others

should have more than they wanted, and me nothin'. But it's small use talkin' to you as takes life so easy, and never has a thought or a wish save for your fisher's life. You don't hardly know what envy means."

"Don't I!" exclaimed Charlie, recalling the feelings with which he had watched the *Sea Gull* glide across the sun-lit bay on the afternoon on which this tale introduced him to our readers, and when his good mother's words reproved him, and set him thinking.

"Don't I!" he repeated emphatically. "Why, Darley, I was dreadful envious of the young Squire myself, and thought it very hard that he should be so well off, while I had to work all the time—and me a lad too, and no older nor him—but mother she spoke to me, very quiet and gentle, but very true too, and showed me as I was wrong. And afterwards, who should I meet but you and Joe, which you both spoke so about Mr. Claude, and looked so dark and so cruel, while you talked of him, that I says to myself, 'If *this* is envy, it's a very wicked and a very dangerous thing, and the less you suffer it in your heart, Charlie Walter, the better!' And then I come to know Mr. Claude, and instead of a

G

proud young gentleman, he was that kind and gentle, as won my heart. And then he wanted to help the poor folks, and began to visit among them, and you'd see what the people in the cottages would say about him now, if you was to ask them. I tell you, Darley, the young Squire don't think a bit more of himself for bein' rich, but he wants to be like the Master what went about doin' good."

"The Master! and pray who's that?" questioned Darley, who had really listened attentively since Charlie had mentioned his own envy of Claude. "Seems as if the young Squire couldn't hev a master, save p'raps old Squire Rivington, and I never heard of his goin' about much doin' good."

"No, Darley, the Master's a greater than that," replied Charlie. "His Master is mine, too, and will be yours if you'll let Him; the best, the kindest, the forgivingest, the loving-est of all masters and friends."

"I never!" said Darley, quite carried away by the boy's enthusiasm. "Who is it now?"

"The Lord Jesus Christ," responded Charlie, solemnly; "and be sure, Darley, no one else could have put it into the heart of anybody

to be so good to you as Mr. Claude has been.
Have you never thought what he's been doin'
for you, and all this too after what you'd tried
to do to him?   But he's learned all this from
his Master, whose servant and child he is."

Darley made no reply, except to mutter to
himself, " Jesus Christ! I han't thought of
Him since I were a boy!" and Charlie,
thinking that enough had been said for once,
took up his cap, and went away, feeling, however, that something had been gained, for not
only had Black Darley been talking freely
and openly—for him—but he had also been
listening, and thus preparing the way maybe
for Claude's next visit.

" Have you heard the news?" asked Mrs.
Darley of Mrs. Walter one evening, when
the two women had met at the grocer's shop
in the town.   A neighbour was sitting with
Darley, so that his wife was able to be out
for an hour.

" News! No; what news?" asked Mrs.
Walter.

" Why, the Squire has bought the Wavebury Arms, and is goin' to turn it into a
Temperance Coffee House, with a readin'
room free for workin' men.   And of all the

blessin's that ever was, that'll be the greatest
for this neighbourhood."

" A blessin'! I should think so indeed!"
replied Mrs. Walter. "The great trouble with
half the people here is just drink. One gets
into the way of it so mighty easy, and out of it
so powerful hard, and I know, for John and me
used to do like our neighbours once. But now
we've been total abstainers for sixteen year
and more, and Charlie he haven't never been
anything else, bless him! and such a healthy,
hearty lad! No one can't say as want of beer
and such like has made him poor or weak."

" No, that's true," replied Mrs. Darley;
"and he's as good and kind as he is strong
and hearty; he's a fine fellow to have for a
son, Mrs. Walter, and you're a happy mother.
But, speakin' of the drink, it's been a fearful
temptation to more than one I could mention,
as has never got on in life, and almost all
through this." And she sighed as she re-
membered her husband, and how he had, in
time past, frequented the Wavebury Arms,
drinking up the earnings which could have
supported them both in comfort.

" And who's to take care of the place, and
keep up the business?" asked Mrs. Walter.

"That ain't known yet," replied Mrs. Darley, "and more, it hasn't even been hinted, and folks says it's a secret as only the Squire himself knows."

"Ah, well," said Mrs. Walter, "they're sure to be good people, whoever's put into a place like that, and it'll be a great blessin' and a comfort to us all;" and there was a hearty ring in the good woman's voice, and a light in her eyes, that showed how truly she rejoiced at the welcome news.

"I quite agree with you, Mrs. Walter," said a manly voice, from behind. "I quite agree with you that they're sure to be good people!" And turning, Mrs. Walter saw Squire Rivington himself, who had come in to give some orders at the grocer's (for he liked to encourage the Wavebury tradesmen), and had heard a part of the conversation. Evidently it had amused him a good deal, for he smiled and even chuckled to himself as he left the shop, while Mrs. Walter exchanged a half-puzzled, half-pleased glance with Mrs. Darley, and said: "Did you ever? And how affable and nice he said it too! How good and kind the Squire and Mr. Claude is growin', to be sure!"

CHAPTER IX.

A TRUE STORY.

THE Waverbury Arms, which long had been a source of evil to the town of Wavebury, was fast becoming an object of absorbing interest and inquisitive inquiry.

Workmen from London had come down to put it into thorough repair, to throw two rooms into one for the reading saloon, to repaint and repaper the whole house, to put in better windows, and rebuild the kitchen range, and do numberless odds and ends which would make the place look absolutely fresh and new.

And while all this was going on, Black Darley was making slow progress towards recovery, and though not convalescent by any means, was yet in a fair way to become so before very long.

Claude paid him a visit about two days after Charlie had been there—as recorded in the last chapter—and was agreeably surprised to find a slight change in the hitherto disagreeable patient. Claude fancied (and yet it could hardly be fancy either) that the man was gentler, less abrupt, less surly and thankless than he had seen him before ; so that the lad took courage presently, and said, " And now, Darley, as it's dull for you lying here, wouldn't you like me to tell you a story ? It shall be a true story, if you like. May I tell it ?"

" Will it be about your Master ?" asked Darley. " Charlie Walter said you had one, which His name were Jesus Christ."

" Yes," said Claude, his whole face lighting up, as he saw the way prepared by his friend, and made easy before him. " Yes, Darley ; Charlie and I have the same blessed Master, and I'm going to tell you about Him You've been a seaman, haven't you now Darley ?"

" Rather, sir," replied the man. " I were a sailor first, and went a many voyages, and then I married and settled down here as fisherman; and maybe I should have done pretty fair, hadn't it been for drink; but that's neither here nor there!"

"Well, Darley, since you've been a sailor and a fisherman, you know what it is to be out all night long with the wind dead against you, and not to be able to get to where you want to go."

"Ay, ay, sir; I know that well enough."

"Well, once upon a time, a very great many years ago, some men put off in a boat to go to the other side of a lake big enough to be a sea.

"But one of their party had been left behind on shore. He was a strange man, with a wonderful power for doing gracious and marvellous things, and with such a loving, tender heart, that the people who knew Him best, loved Him dearly, and even those who knew Him very little, and only perhaps brought their sick to be healed by Him (for He cured the sick better than any doctor) could see that He was not a common man.

"Now, not being a common man, and being able, too, to cure the sick, and heal the maimed, and give sight to the blind, you may be sure lots of folks came about Him, and He was kept busy healing some and teaching others."

"Well, yes; that's nought but nat'ral," remarked Darley.

"Yes," resumed Claude; "but at last the people who had been with Him a long time (some of them had come from a distance, too) grew faint and hungry, and having fed them with a little food which He had by Him, but which proved enough, after all, for the whole multitude, the Teacher sent them all away to their homes, while His friends (as I began by telling you) sailed off in their boat, and He Himself went up into a mountain, to pray and to be quiet after the work and trials of the day.

"But the little ship with the fishermen in it (did I tell you they were fishermen, Darley ?) was now far out to sea, and tossing about on the waves. It was no use to spread the sail, for the wind was contrary, so the poor fellows rowed and rowed, hoping to make the land.

"And in the night—this dark, windy, boisterous night at sea—they saw a strange and wonderful sight; a sight that no one had ever seen before, and that no one has ever seen since."

"And what were that?" asked Darley, whose eyes were fixed on Claude in evident interest.

"They saw the figure of a man coming along towards them on the water; not swimming, not flying like a gull, but just walking, as though the waves were a solid floor."

"Oh my!" ejaculated Darley.

"Well, you can understand," continued the young Squire, "that these poor fishers were frightened, and they called out that it was a ghost. But even while they so feared and cried out, a sweet voice that they well knew came to them over the water, saying, 'Be of good cheer, it is I; be not afraid!'"

"And then?" questioned Darley eagerly.

"Then," resumed Claude, "one of the fishermen, whose name was Peter, called out, 'Lord, if it be Thou, bid me come to Thee on the water.' And immediately the voice answered, 'Come.'"

"You don't mean for to tell me as he were cracked enough to go?" said Black Darley incredulously. "It may be all **very** well for ghostesses, and such like, but for a fisherman—but no—he surely didn't?"

"Ah, Darley, faith and love will do wonders. Peter could not but obey that dearly loved voice. He threw himself out of the boat, and walked on the water to meet his Lord. He believed in the power and goodness of his Master, and while his faith was strong, he imitated Him and walked on the water, the waves bearing him up. But suddenly he looked round, he saw and felt how hard the wind was blowing, and that the waves were high, with angry white crests; and as he did so, he took his eyes off his Lord, he ceased to think of the Lord's love and wonderful power. And in *that minute* he began to sink. He felt the water, at first so firm under his feet, rush over them, and then he knew that he was going down, down."

"He should have took a breaster, and struck out," said Darley.

"He did what was better," responded Claude. "He called to his Master in his terror and despair, 'Lord, save me!' And immediately his Master put forth His hand (that dear, kind hand which had so often healed the sick, and raised the fallen, and even given life to the dead) and caught him and said to him, 'O thou of little faith, wherefore didst thou doubt?' And when Peter and his Lord got into the ship, the wind ceased."

"And that there's a true story?" asked Darley.

"Quite true," replied Claude.

"But you said you'd tell me, sir, about *your* Master," said Darley; "and here you've been a-tellin' about somebody else as were the Master of Peter and some other fellows."

"But what if it were all the same, Darley? What if my Master is the very One of whom I have been telling you—the very One who did so much good among the poor and sick, those hundreds of years ago; and walked on the water and saved Peter from sinking? I tell you, Darley, He, and He only, is *my* Master, and Charlie Walter's Master, and the Master and dear Friend of every one who truly loves and wishes to serve Him. And believe me, Darley, He is as ready to save every one from the great flood of their sins now, as He was to save poor sinking Peter. They have only to cry, from their hearts, ' Lord, save me,' and His hand is at once outstretched. Ah, Darley, none but those who love and have followed the Lord know what it is, in the hour of darkness and trouble, to hear Him say, ' It is I ; be not afraid !' and to feel sure that He who gave His precious life for them on the cross, will love them even to the end, and is able and willing to keep and bless them."

Claude said no more : his earnest desire to say something that would touch Darley's heart—his great longing to win this poor soul for his Master, had made his voice tremble, and his eyes grow dim and misty. He got up from his seat now, and went away; and as he walked homeward, he thanked God and took courage, for though in much weakness and in fear, the precious seed of the kingdom had been sown, he knew that heaven's sunshine and heaven's rain— the life-giving power of the Eternal Spirit— could quicken that seed and cause it to spring and grow, and bear fruit. And his heart, in the fulness of its yearning, cried out, " Lord, let it be so unto Thy servant, for Thine own mercy's sake, and for the honour of Thy great name."

CHAPTER X.

"NOT YET."

I F ever Charlie Walter had been tempted to pride, it was on account of his health and strength. There was not a lad in Wavebury so tall and strong for his age; not a lad who could do what he could, or endure so much fatigue and hardship. In rowing, in swimming, in all things requiring strength and vigour as well as skill, he was first; and his mother had often told her neighbours that her Charlie had never had an illness in all his life.

But no one, even the most healthy, can

insure himself against the invasion of disease, and Charlie had yet to learn that even youthful vigour is only too easily undermined by sickness. It was not Charlie's fault that he had to be out the whole of one night in a cold wet fog; out all night in an open boat on the sea, and in a fog that turned to sleet towards morning, which chilled the lad to the bone, and sent him home—when he landed —with his teeth chattering, and his whole frame shaking with cold.

Mrs. Walter made him go to bed, and gave him some hot herb tea, but fever succeeded the shivering, and soon Charlie was so very ill that the doctor had to be sent for.

Claude soon heard of his friend's illness, and came daily to inquire about him; but Charlie was delirious and in a stupor by turns, rarely knowing any one, or being conscious of anything that was going on about him.

Now he would fancy himself in the cave at Agate Bay, and would mutter scraps of the conversation which had there taken place between Joe and Darley; or he would think that he was swimming and making for the shore near the cutting, and would strike out with arms and legs as though wrestling with the waves. And then again he would imagine himself talking with Claude, and would say, "Yes, sir, it's quite true; I *did* envy you once; but all the envy's gone out of me long ago, and I love you now—so dearly—oh, so dearly. I'd give my life for yours free and willin', sir—I would indeed!"

And all this went on over and over again, as the crisis drew near, the critical time which would show whether this dear, brave boy was to live—to live, or to die.

"How is he?" asked Claude of John Walter, who opened the cottage door to him one evening.

John looked very worn and sad, and he shook his head despondingly as he replied, "No better, sir, no better; on the contrary, sir, he seems to get worse and worse. An hour or two ago he was talkin' and ravin', and throwin' hisself about, but now he's lyin' kind of stupid like, with his eyes, that was so bright, half open and dull—almost as though he was gone already. Oh, sir, he's my only son, my right hand, and the very light of his mother's eyes, and it takes well-nigh more faith than I've got—though I've trusted the Lord all my life—to say, 'Thy will be done!' I doubt, sir, if that boy's took, it will be the death-blow to wife and me."

Claude's eyes were brimful of tears, and he could not speak a word to comfort the old fisherman; but he wrung his hand, and then passed into the bedroom where lay the friend to whom he owed so much.

Mrs. Walter was standing by the bed. She placed a finger upon her lips as Claude entered; he stepped softly to her side, understanding that the crisis was close at hand— the terrible moment, the issue of which none could foretell.

As though spell-bound, the two watchers stood waiting. Charlie lay quite still, seeming hardly to breathe; his thick brown curls disordered, his eyes and lips half open. This continued for perhaps half an hour. Then, all at once, there was a movement in the prostrate figure. The sick boy half raised himself, his eyes opened wide, and flashed with a sudden brilliancy, his thin arms stretched themselves out.

"My golden ship!" he cried, such a thrill in his voice that Claude started. Then, in earnest, plaintive tones, while a look of love and longing stole over his wasted features, the words came slowly, one by one : " Lord, if it be Thou, bid me come to Thee on the water ! "

There was a pause, as though the sick lad's spirit were only awaiting the permission of the Saviour to leave its earthly dwelling. An eager, attentive, listening expression took possession of the face.   Then it faded out, and Charlie sank back on his pillow sighing, " Not yet ! not yet !   The Lord says wait ! "

Once more there was silence for some minutes.   Then the sweet dark eyes opened once more, but slowly and naturally this time ; and the old loving, tender voice murmured weakly, but in tones of unmistakable recognition, "Mother ! "   And as Mrs. Walter bent over her boy, Claude Rivington, with one great sob that would not be repressed, dropped on his knees by the bedside, and poured out his heart in silent thanksgiving.

But it must not be imagined that during this time of Charlie's sickness Black Darley was forgotten.   Claude still visited him daily, sent him all that was necessary to nourish and strengthen him, paid the rent of his

house, and did all in his power to win this
rough, hard man to a love of goodness and
truth.

As for Mrs. Darley, she was a source of
constant wonder to Claude. He had heard
from others, not from her—how her husband
had abused and ill-treated her for years, and
yet how she had never attempted to leave
him; never even complained of him; and
now she tended him as lovingly, nursed him
as tenderly, as though he had ever proved
himself a pattern husband, all that was kind
and considerate and unselfish.

When he spoke roughly, she answered
him gently; when he grumbled and scolded,
she bore it silently. Verily this poor creature
had learned lessons of meekness and Christian forbearance in the heavy trials that had
fallen to her lot.

After telling Darley the story from the
Gospel, as we recorded it in a previous
chapter, Claude had thought it well not to
refer to it again, nor to repeat the experiment
unless he were asked to do so.

He knew that with a man like Darley,
any change in him—if change there was to
be—must be very gradual; and to try and

hurry it might be only to hinder the work in his heart.

Still, though little was said, Claude thought that in some ways, small in themselves, but important as showing the course that the man's thoughts and feelings were taking, Darley's character was undergoing a change, none the less sure for being slow.

How true it is that the kingdom of God in the heart cometh not with observation; and now even Claude's earnest, prayerful watching, could only detect occasionally these faint signs that the labour of love had not all been thrown away, but that this man's heart, grown hard and callous in sin, had yet been touched with the finger of Almighty love and grace.

Certainly Darley's manner was not so surly and churlish as it had been hitherto. He now answered respectfully when Claude spoke to him, and he had even thanked him once or twice in a curious, awkward, shame-faced way, for his kindness.

To his wife, too, he was far less harsh, and he actually went so far on one occasion as to tell her that something she had cooked for him was "oncommon good."

The flush of proud happiness—of glad sur-prise—that came over her wan cheeks at his scanty praise, showed how unused she was to anything beside hard words and fault-finding.

Darley saw the flush, saw it brighten up the pale, sorrowful countenance which had once attracted him by its simple beauty, and sweet, confiding expression, and it recalled to his mind the old days, when as a young man he courted her, and made all those golden promises, not one of which he had kept.

One day, as his eyes followed her about their poor room, watching how loosely her old gown hung about the shrunken shoulders, once so plump and shapely, how careworn and how weary she looked, a pang shot through his heart such as he had never felt before. Had this ill-used, neglected, wronged wife of his ever resented his cruel treatment of her? he asked himself. Had she ever given blow for blow, taunt for taunt, neglect and unkindness in return for his? And his newly awakened conscience could not but answer, " Never; no, never!" and his heart softened more and more towards the faithful creature who had clung to him through every-thing without even a reproach.

So that when she returned to his side, and stooped over him to smooth the bed-clothes, he looked up suddenly into her face, saying, "Somehow, Nancy, I've been thinkin' over the old times when we began life together, and the little 'un we lost—and—and—if you don't mind, kiss me, wife, as you used when we was a-courtin ; kiss me, Nancy, will you ?"

"Will I ? Oh, Blake, oh, my darlin', my darlin' ! Oh, thank God ! thank God !" and the husband and wife, for the first time for years, were clasped in each other's arms ; and Claude, who had entered at that moment, turned away, and went silently out ; the place, poor as it was, had become holy ground, made sacred by the reunion of two long-severed hearts ; and he softly closed the door, and left them to their happiness.

CHAPTER XI.

THE SQUIRE'S SECRET REVEALED.

HARLIE'S convalescence was far more rapid than that of Darley. Here his young vigorous life and temperate habits gave him the advantage over the man who had weakened his constitution in time past by his excesses.

Still, Darley was improving fast now, and had even been out for half an hour's drive in Claude's little pony-carriage, in which the young Squire delighted to give his "patients," as he called them, an airing.

Nor was it only in body that Darley was improving day by day,—very slowly, indeed almost imperceptibly at first, the light had dawned upon him; and even after he knew the right, and had strong desires to do it, the thought of all he should have to give up,— his drink, his evil companions, the pleasures —such as they were—of the past, had kept him from the surrender of his heart to Christ, from the utterance of the cry, " Lord, save me !"

But the love that had so freely been shown him triumphed at last, and across the stormy waves of his sins and his sorrow—with the winds of temptation blowing about him— this disciple, only just learning to recognise the Master's voice and to desire His presence, walked to meet Jesus.

" I'd like to ask your advice, if you please, sir, if I might make so bold," said Darley to Claude, some little time after the events recorded in the last chapter.

" My advice is quite at your service, Darley; if you want it upon any subject that I understand."

" Well, sir, you see, thanks to all the care I've had, I'm a-gettin' well rapid, and I've been thinkin' I ought for to be lookin' out for somethin' to do. Here's me and Nancy been livin' on charity for this two months and more, and I'll never be able to thank you for all you've done for me, sir, more ways nor one. But I must be on the look out for work of some sort, though I'm afeared I ain't quite strong enough to begin it afore the new year."

"No," replied Claude, "you will do very well if you can commence steady work then."

"I don't want to take to fishin' again, sir," continued Darley; "our boat was sold before Joe went away, and I don't think I should care to have the old life all over once more. A fisherman's temptations is terrible, special to drink, when he gets chilled and wet, and feels kind of faint and tired, for want of warm food, and his night's sleep. And yet I don't feel no wish to leave Wavebury neither, if I can find somethin' to do here, for while I've been laid up, and everybody's been so good to me and Nance, I've come to be that partial to the place as I never thought it were in me to be. But I'd be glad to hear your opinion, sir, and would take it grateful."

"I will speak to my father about it, Darley; he is always ready to give his advice and his help; and should I hear of a situation for you, or have anything to propose to you, I will come and tell you at once."

"Thank you kindly, sir; and now please,

sir, if it ain't a-troublin' of you too much, will you, when you call here next, sir, bring with you that there big dog of your'n as bit me? Poor brute, he were only a-doin' of his dooty faithful and true, and now I've made peace with God and man, I don't want to hev *one* enemy."

Claude smiled.

"You need not even put it off until I call next time, unless you want to do so," said he pleasantly. "He is waiting for me quite quietly and patiently outside your door at this very moment, and he has often carried for me the little baskets and parcels containing things for you. I do not think you will find, Darley, that Champion has any ill-will towards you; I am not afraid to trust him."

So saying, Claude stepped to the door and called the dog in.

"Come here, Champion," said he; and as Darley put out his great hand, and stroked and patted the creature's handsome head, the noble animal acknowledged the courtesy by extending his huge paw in token of friendly feeling.

"There!—he never does that of his own accord unless he means to be friends with a person," said Claude ; " so all is right between you two."

Claude was as good as his word, and a talk with his father resulted in a place being offered to Darley, of under gardener at the Hall —a post which he most thankfully accepted. As for Mrs. Darley, a new life had already begun for her, and sometimes her husband, when he looked at her, could not but wonder, for the old bloom was returning to her cheeks, the old brightness to her eyes ; and, in spite of the years of sorrow and trial, she was beginning to look quite young and pretty, through sheer happiness and rest of heart, so that Black Darley—well, Black Darley just fell in love with his wife all over again, and more thoroughly than ever he did in her young days.

Meanwhile, the town was full of wonder and gossip about the Wavebury Arms. Parts of it had been rebuilt ; handsome windows had been put in ; the garden had been enlarged and properly laid out, and some trees had been planted.

Everything looked bright and new, and a report had gone about that at Christmas or New Year the place would be opened ; and many hearts that had mourned over the evils of the Wavebury Arms, looked forward with genuine thankfulness to the carrying out of the Squire's new plan for improving the condition of the people, and for stemming the tide of drunkenness which was the curse of the place.

But there was one thing which puzzled the simple folk very much.

Though it was perfectly understood that the old name of the Wavebury Arms was to be discontinued, it did not yet appear what name should take its place.

The Squire and his son were supposed to know, of course; but if they did, they made no confidants, and the name of the new coffee house remained a mystery.

Christmas Day brought more than usual rejoicings this year.

Hitherto, the Squire had given to a few old favourites of his wife, among the poorer people, meat and coals at Christmas time, more, however, in remembrance of her, than for a festive keeping of the great day. But this year the gladness was general, for the Squire opened his great big servants' hall from one to five on Christmas Day; and there was the grand old English dinner of roast beef and plum pudding going all the time, with plenty of tea and coffee; and any one that wished might come in and dine.

Then, on the next evening, there was a big Christmas tree for all the poor children, and presents of warm clothing and pretty books and toys and sweetmeats, to say nothing of oranges and nuts in abundance. And Squire Rivington himself came in, accompanied by his son, and patted the children's heads, and kissed some of the babies, and helped to distribute the gifts, and was just about as happy as the little ones themselves, and that was saying a great deal. But, in spite of the great Christmas feast, and the general merry·making, and the Squire's warm welcome and kind words and affable manners, no one could find out anything (though many tried) about the name of the coffee house, or who were to be its tenants.

On New Year's Eve, however, at about seven o'clock, the Squire's close carriage drew up at John Walter's door, and Claude jumped out.

"John," said he, "and you, Mrs. Walter, and you, Charlie, must get ready at once, and come with me. You must ask no questions but wrap up warmly, for the night is cold. You're sure you feel well enough to venture, dear Charlie?" and when Charlie, much astonished, replied, "Oh yes, sir, thank you, I'm quite well," Claude helped to wrap him up, and then the four got into the carriage, and drove down the cliff road, through the town, till they stopped before what had once been the Wavebury Arms.

The Walter family stood petrified with astonishment as they alighted from the carriage; for there before them was the most cheerful, inviting sight. Through the bright windows the lights burned clear; the ruddy fires flashed and glowed. In the kitchen they could see the new pans and the other cooking utensils hanging on the wall, or neatly standing on shelves. The reading-room was brilliantly lighted, and full of great book cupboards, and tables and chairs. This room occupied the whole width of the front, on the second floor, and in large letters across the central window were the words—

"JOHN WALTER AND SON."

But what arrested Charlie's attention, almost

at first, and sent a glad flush into his white cheeks, was the sign of the house. It hung out over the front door, and consisted of a large transparency with a lighted gas jet behind. The transparency represented a vessel bathed in sunset hues, and sailing over a sea flooded with light, while underneath were the words—

"My Golden Ship."

"Yes," said Claude, as his friend, unable to speak, looked to him for an explanation. "It means that my father begs your parents and you to accept this house and business, and do us the favour of keeping it up, thus helping us to encourage temperance and right feeling and self-improvement among the townspeople of our little Wavebury."

Then, as John and Mrs. Walter turned to cross the threshold of their new home, where the Squire stood smiling and ready to receive them, Claude grasped Charlie's hand in his, and said,—

"Charlie, had it not been for you, I should probably never have thought about good things, or learned to love Jesus. Your dream has come true, and you have been the means of leading me to Him. Let this Golden Ship remind you, dear friend, of all that has passed between us. As for me, I need no reminder, for how can I forget what I owe you? You saved my life, Charlie, and, what is far more, you were the instrument in God's hands for the saving of my soul. You taught me how to be happy here, and how I may look forward, through Christ, to far greater happiness at last in the world to come. God bless you; God for ever bless and keep you—Charlie, dear Charlie!"

And with these words the young Squire and the young fisherman—hand in hand—entered together

"My Golden Ship."

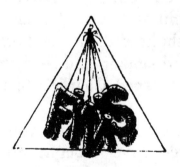

Butler & Tanner, Frome, and London.